EMOTIONAL INTELLIGENCE
skills assessment

EiSA

Self

Steven J. Stein
Derek Mann
Peter Papadogiannis

Pfeiffer
A Wiley Imprint
www.pfeiffer.com

MHS

Emotional Intelligence
Assessments and Solutions

Published by Pfeiffer
An Imprint of Wiley.
989 Market Street, San Francisco, CA 94103-1741
www.pfeiffer.com

Readers should be aware that Internet websites offered as citations and/or sources for further information may have changed or disappeared between the time this was written and when it is read.

For additional copies/bulk purchases of this book in the U.S. please contact 800-274-4434.

Pfeiffer books and products are available through most bookstores. To contact Pfeiffer directly call our Customer Care Department within the U.S. at 800-274-4434, outside the U.S. at 317-572-3985, fax 317-572-4002, or visit www.pfeiffer.com.

Pfeiffer also publishes its books in a variety of electronic formats. Some content that appears in print may not be available in electronic books.

Deluxe Set ISBN: 978-0-470-49944-3

Set ISBN: 978-0-470-46241-6

Self ISBN: 978-0-470-24865-2

Acquiring Editor: Holly J. Allen

Marketing Manager: Tolu Babalola

Director of Development: Kathleen Dolan Davies

Developmental Editor: Susan Rachmeler

Editorial Assistant: Dani Scoville

Production Editor: Michael Kay

Editor: Rebecca Taff

Manufacturing Supervisor: Becky Morgan

Composition: Classic Typography

Design: Adrian Morgan and Gearbox

Printed in the United States of America

Printing   SKY10098501_021725

Instructions

The EISA: Self consists of fifty items designed to assess emotional intelligence in adults. Please read each statement carefully and select the response from the following 5-point scale that best represents how often this statement is true of you:

1 = Very seldom or not true of me

2 = Seldom true of me

3 = Sometimes true of me

4 = Often true of me

5 = Very often true of me or true of me

Record your response on the line to the left of each item. Please respond to all items; do not leave any items blank.

_____ 1. When faced with a difficult situation, I like to collect all the information about it that I can.

_____ 2. It is a problem controlling my anger.

_____ 3. I am attuned to other people's reactions to me.

_____ 4. It's hard for me to smile.

_____ 5. I feel sure of myself in most situations.

_____ 6. I tend to exaggerate.

_____ 7. I believe in my ability to achieve what I set out to achieve.

_____ 8. When upset I often lose control.

_____ 9. I often feel anxious when working toward a meaningful goal.

_____ 10. My approach in overcoming difficulties is to move step by step.

_____ 11. I'm in touch with my emotions.

_____ 12. In the past few years I've accomplished little.

_____ 13. I am easily distracted by things going on around me.

_____ 14. When trying to solve a problem, I look at each possibility and then decide on the best way.

_____ 15. I'm impatient.

_____ 16. When facing a problem, the first thing I do is stop and think.

_____ 17. Even when upset, I'm aware of what's happening to me.

_____ 18. I like to get an overview of a problem before trying to solve it.

_____ 19. My impulsiveness creates problems.

_____ 20. I am assertive.

1 = Very seldom or not true of me

2 = Seldom true of me

3 = Sometimes true of me

4 = Often true of me

5 = Very often true of me or true of me

_____ 21. I'm sensitive to the feelings of others.

_____ 22. I am good at perceiving the emotions of others.

_____ 23. I have good self-respect.

_____ 24. I am often told to lower my voice during discussions.

_____ 25. I am aware of how I feel.

_____ 26. It's difficult for me to stand up for my rights.

_____ 27. People gravitate toward me.

_____ 28. I'm unable to show affection.

_____ 29. I lack self-confidence.

_____ 30. Even when upset I can stay focused on the task at hand.

_____ 31. I'm aware of the way I feel.

_____ 32. I get carried away with my imagination and fantasies.

_____ 33. I really don't know what I'm good at.

_____ 34. I'm good at understanding the way other people feel.

_____ 35. I've got a bad temper.

_____ 36. I know how to keep calm in difficult situations.

_____ 37. I tend to explode with anger easily.

_____ 38. I have good relations with others.

_____ 39. I don't feel good about myself.

_____ 40. In handling situations that arise, I try to think of as many approaches as I can.

_____ 41. I process all relevant facts when making a decision.

_____ 42. It's hard for me to keep things in the proper perspective.

_____ 43. I misperceive other people's emotions.

_____ 44. It's hard for me to make decisions on my own.

_____ 45. I can remain composed even in the most difficult situations.

1 = Very seldom or not true of me

2 = Seldom true of me

3 = Sometimes true of me

4 = Often true of me

5 = Very often true of me or true of me

_____ 46. I can control the outward expression of my emotions.

_____ 47. It's hard for me to understand the way I feel.

_____ 48. I modify my emotions to enhance my decision making.

_____ 49. I'm impulsive.

_____ 50. It's hard for me to describe my feelings.

Scoring

Instructions: Transfer your scores from your assessment into the grid below. For each numbered item, place your score in the highlighted box. If the corresponding box for the item is shaded gray, use the reverse response shown in the key, rather than your original response. Thus, if you scored yourself a 5, for a reverse-scored item, you'd enter a 1 in the box.

When you've entered all of your scores, sum each column to find the subtotal score for each factor. Then add each factor's subtotal scores together and record this number in the total box for each factor.

Reverse Key

If the box for an item is light gray, use the reverse score as shown below:

Original Response	Reverse Response
1	5
2	4
3	3
4	2
5	1

Item	Perceiving	Managing	Decision Making	Achieving	Influencing
1					
2					
3					
4					
5					
6					
7					
8					
9					
10					
11					
12					
13					
14					
15					
16					
17					
18					
19					
20					
21					
22					
23					
24					
25					
Subtotals					

Item	Perceiving	Managing	Decision Making	Achieving	Influencing
26					
27					
28					
29					
30					
31					
32					
33					
34					
35					
36					
37					
38					
39					
40					
41					
42					
43					
44					
45					
46					
47					
48					
49					
50					
Subtotals					
Totals					

To calculate your standardized score for each of the factors, copy your total score for each factor into the appropriate Step 1 of each of the formula groupings below. Then complete the sequence of calculations to arrive at your standardized score.

Perceiving

Step 1: Perceiving Total Score = _____ (A)

Step 2: (A) – 43.14 = _____ (B)

Step 3: (B) / 7.28 = _____ (C)

Step 4: (C) + 5 = _____ (standard score)

Managing

Step 1: Managing Total Score = _____ (A)

Step 2: (A) – 33.90 = _____ (B)

Step 3: (B) / 6.13 = _____ (C)

Step 4: (C) + 5 = _____ (standard score)

Decision Making

Step 1: DM Total Score = _____ (A)

Step 2: (A) – 34.14 = _____ (B)

Step 3: (B) / 3.83 = _____(C)

Step 4: (C) + 5 = _____ (standard score)

Achieving

Step 1: Achieving Total Score = _____ (A)

Step 2: (A) – 28.46 = _____ (B)

Step 3: (B) / 5.68 = _____ (C)

Step 4: (C) + 5 = _____ (standard score)

Influencing

Step 1: Influencing Total Score = _____ (A)

Step 2: (A) – 32.01 = _____(B)

Step 3: (B) / 7.40 = _____ (C)

Step 4: (C) + 5 = _____ (standard score)

Write your standard score for each factor in the boxes labeled "Self" below. Then draw a bar on the graph the length of that number:

Perceiving	Self:					
Managing	Self:					
Decision Making	Self:					
Achieving	Self:					
Influencing	Self:					
	0	2	4	6	8	10

The higher your score, the more frequently you tend to utilize that factor.

Perceiving

The ability to accurately recognize, attend to, and understand emotion.

Decision Making

The appropriate application of emotion to manage change and solve problems.

Achieving

The ability to generate the necessary emotions to self-motivate in the pursuit of realistic and meaningful objectives.

Influencing

The ability to recognize, manage, and evoke emotion within oneself and others to promote change.

Managing

The ability to effectively manage, control, and express emotions.

Perceiving

The ability to accurately recognize, attend to, and understand emotion.

Write your standard score for this factor in the box labeled "Self" below. Then draw a bar on the graph the length of that number.

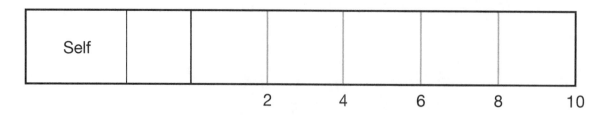

Perceiving emotions is the ability to be aware of, understand, and pay attention to emotions. Emotions contain valuable information about other people, relationships, and our surroundings. The ability to perceive emotions starts with being aware of emotional signals, accurately identifying what they mean, and then applying them to a given situation. The better someone is at reading and understanding emotions, the more appropriately that person will be able to respond.

The Perceiving factor of the EISA also deals with the consequences of being unable to or unwilling to use feelings and mood to guide subsequent behavior.

People skilled in emotional perception are successful because:

- The ability to discern between emotions and their degrees of intensity allows people to better manage interpersonal relationships. This skill is especially important in environments that are constantly changing or are emotionally charged.

- Being able to describe and identify emotions provides more opportunities to be influential. People who are able to sufficiently appraise and describe their own emotions are more likely to exhibit more positive emotions and less non-verbal anger. This ability allows you to be perceived as more socially attractive and less avoidant.

- The capacity to perceive and respond appropriately to the emotions of others is important to a person's overall performance. Being able to consciously interpret the group's tone, body language, and degree of eye contact gives a person a higher sense of awareness. For example, if a group that you belong to is fearful of making a change, you are more likely to be able to recognize the need for an empathic or motivational conversation.

- Being authentic and predictable in the expression of emotions is a key to success when interacting in groups. Highly perceptive individuals often obtain full commitment from the groups that they associate with because they are aware of how positive and negative emotions can increase or decrease individual and group morale.

- Emotionally predictable people are often more successful because they are better at recognizing their emotional triggers. Being aware of emotional triggers helps people stay calm, which often produces a higher level of trust and cooperation from others.

Managing

The ability to effectively manage, control, and express emotions.

Write your standard score for this factor in the box labeled "Self" below. Then draw a bar on the graph the length of that number.

This skill represents a willingness and ability to be aware of, evaluate, and adequately control the emotions necessary for effective functioning. Managing emotions, which includes the ability to appraise emotions swiftly and accurately, is a critical component of emotional intelligence. A more developed EI translates into a more accurate appraisal of one's own emotions, which permits enhanced processing and greater expression of those emotions to others. It is this level of processing that is so vital to the success of subsequent interpersonal interactions.

People skilled in emotional management are successful because:

- The ability to manage emotions can translate into an accurate interpretation of an individual's own emotions and the emotions of others. Skilled emotional managers are better equipped to express those emotions to others. It is this level of ability that is so vital to the quality of interpersonal interactions.

- Managing your emotions helps harness the energy needed to sustain motivation, cope with stress, and make decisions. For example, the expression of a positive emotion is a good indication that all is well, while the expression of a negative emotion can suggest the need for deliberation and attention to detail.

- People are often faced with personal, social, and professional situations in which family members, friends, clients, or colleagues become emotionally charged, allowing their emotional experience to overly influence thoughts, decisions, and actions. Using emotional skills (e.g., attending to body language, tone of voice, and so forth) helps manage the situation and put others at ease, which can help productivity and long-term success.

- Being able to manage one's own emotions, including the ability to express these emotions, can lead to the development of more meaningful interpersonal relationships. For example, preventing emotional outbursts due to insignificant or trivial concerns or empathizing with someone who has had a bad day can lead to deeper emotional connections and greater interpersonal satisfaction.

- Individuals who recognize when they feel frustrated, sad, irritable, or elated, and perceive how these feelings alter their behavior are often viewed as empathic, composed, and socially attractive, which can lead to greater personal and professional opportunities.

Decision Making

The application of emotion to manage change and solve problems.

Write your standard score for this factor in the box labeled "Self" below. Then draw a bar on the graph the length of that number.

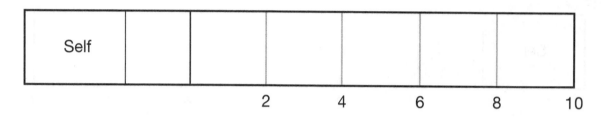

The process of decision making requires the attention to and processing of relevant environmental, intra- and interpersonal cues. The mood of the individual coupled with the individual's ability to attend to cues can have a profound impact on his or her decision outcomes. An emotionally intelligent individual is well equipped to recognize the need to engage specific emotions to facilitate the processing of relevant sources of information. In other words, the ability to manage change and solve problems is a reflection of one's ability to match one's emotions with the demands of the situation.

Emotions such as anger, fear, empathy, happiness, and sadness have been shown to modulate the decision-making process. Given the prevalence of these emotions in daily living, the emotionally intelligent individual should possess the ability to successfully recognize and employ these emotions to facilitate the decision-making process.

People skilled in emotional decision making are successful because:

- They possess the ability to successfully recognize when it is necessary to activate an emotion compatible with task demands. For example, decision making in which considerable attention must be given to the details of the existing environment requires a more subdued emotional state.

- They are able to manage change and solve problems of a personal and interpersonal nature based on their emotional state. For example, decision making with a reliance on pre-existing knowledge structures accompanies a positive mood state. In other words, the "gut reaction" approach to decision making often applies in this case.

- They have an astute awareness of the "problem" and are able to pair it with an appropriate emotional state.

Achieving

The ability to generate the necessary emotions to self-motivate in the pursuit of realistic and meaningful objectives.

Write your standard score for this factor in the box labeled "Self" below. Then draw a bar on the graph the length of that number.

People skilled in this area experience more pleasure in success, take greater responsibility for the outcomes of their own actions, enjoy activities with moderate levels of risk, and prefer feedback. Individuals who maintain a task orientation and possess confidence in their ability to achieve report better moods and higher social and emotional adjustment.

Motivation has been linked with satisfaction, enjoyment, and interest in life. Individuals with lower motivation tend to have a difficult time adjusting to change and may be more prone to burnout.

People skilled in emotional achievement are successful because they:

- Experience more pleasure in success
- Take greater responsibility for the outcomes of their own actions
- Prefer to know about the level of their success and/or failures immediately
- Enjoy moderate levels of risk
- Demonstrate fewer and weaker physiological symptoms of arousal (that is, rising heart rate and blood pressure)
- Naturally find ways to make most tasks personally relevant and meaningful. This intrinsic motivation results in the experience of positive emotions that often result in increased optimism and effective decision making

Influencing

The ability to recognize, manage, and evoke emotion within oneself and others to promote change.

Write your standard score for this factor in the box labeled "Self" below. Then draw a bar on the graph the length of that number.

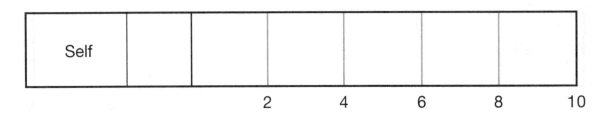

Emotions play an enormous role in the creation and maintenance of social relationships. An individual's emotions are factors that can shape the behaviors, thoughts, and emotions of others through the perception of facial, postural, or verbal information. The most evident influence of emotion in social situations is the capacity to evoke emotions in other people. Inferences made by others based on emotional information can influence power, competence, credibility, and approachability. Emotions that people witness in others may influence their current interactions, as well as future relationships with that person.

The type, frequency, and intensity of expressed emotions can have a profound effect on the depth and breadth of our social relationships, which in turn impacts that amount of social influence someone may have. The expression of emotions plays an important role in the creation of social relationships. An individual's emotions may inspire others to achieve greater goals, influence creativity, and improve collaboration.

People skilled in influencing others are successful because:

- Their awareness of their own strengths provides them with more opportunities to gain influence with others. Consistently putting oneself in an influential position allows others to know what one brings to the table. People are attracted to and motivated to work with someone who believes that he or she can make things happen.

- Being able to assert oneself appropriately often allows people to manage others effectively. Skilled influencers are able to describe what needs to be done, which helps when setting proper direction and tone.

- The ability to use positive emotions (both perception and expression) effectively enhances the influence one has. Skilled influencers often use positive emotions (such as happiness, optimism, a smile) to engage others, which leads to increased approachability and a desire for future relationships. This increases their personal networks and beneficial alliances.

The capacity to employ a positive and confident disposition increases their likelihood of influencing others. Others generally perceive this disposition (in various environments) as energizing and motivating.